easy blues
rhythms for guitar

by Ed Lozano

The fun and simple way to learn the basics of rhythm guitar while playing with a band. Special sections on open-string boogie riffs, two-note chord patterns, turnarounds, and much more.

T0080127

Cover photograph of Gibson L5 by Randall Wallace
courtesy of The Wallace Collection
Author photograph by Scott Abrams
Project editor: Ed Lozano
Interior design and layout: WR Music Service

Order No. AM 971432
US International Standard Book Number: 0.8256.1901.7
UK International Standard Book Number: 0.7119.8979.6

Exclusive Distributors:
Music Sales Corporation
257 Park Avenue South, New York, NY 10010 USA
Music Sales Limited
8/9 Frith Street, London W1D 3JB England
Music Sales Pty. Limited
120 Rothschild Street, Rosebery, Sydney, NSW 2018, Australia

Printed in the United States of America by
Vicks Lithograph and Printing Corporation

Amsco Publications
New York/London/Paris/Sydney/Copenhagen/Madrid

CD Track Listing

Contents

Acknowledgements

I would like to thank:
- Peter Pickow and Dan Earley whose patience, knowledge, and guidance proved invaluable; without their help this book would not have been possible.
- All of the folks at Music Sales Corp.
- My family and friends (you know who you are)
- The countless number of blues musicians whose recordings have been an education and inspiration.
- And finally, to the Creator for all of the above and then some. I humbly gassho before you.

Preface

The blues is an American artform that dates back to the early 1900s. This music style was born out of the desire for true freedom of expression. The themes expressed in this musical style are basic human qualities that people from all walks of life can identify with. The blues is about expressing those basic human emotions that are inside all of us. From the pain of love lost to the joy of love found, from traveling endlessly to finding your way home, "The blues is simply. . . ," as Willie Dixon so eloquently and succinctly put it, ". . . the facts of life."

Every musical genre, from jazz to country to rock and soul, has a direct lineage to the blues. Heavy metal and hip-hop are not immune to the infectious grooves and shuffles while R&B and swing draw directly from its well.

The blues is simple to understand and with a little bit of practice you can begin to master the subtleties that make this music so much fun.

So-whether you're looking to rock, honky-tonk, groove, swing, jam, *etc.*-learning the blues can help you to better express yourself.

① Introduction

Welcome to *Easy Blues Rhythms for Guitar!*

This instruction method has been tried and tested with many students. Some have gone on to play professionally while others have enjoyed the ability to express themselves in front of a few friends and family while still others have simply just entertained themselves.

The music examples are graded beginning with basic rhythms and rests, to open-string boogie patterns, and progressing to more challenging techniques. These examples are clearly demonstrated on the accompanying CD with each idea practiced over one chord. The CD also includes a practice track for you to play along with. All of the examples are then demonstrated in the traditional 12-bar blues form.

There are also sections on turnarounds and two-note chords. Next, the method continues with all of the techniques discussed (and some new ones) in the section, appropriately entitled, "Putting It All Together." Finally, the last section has six different songs demonstrating some advanced techniques.

This method is set up to take the student from basic ideas that are applicable in real-life playing situations to actual riffs and grooves that make up the blues vocabulary.

Easy Blues Rhythms for Guitar, when used in conjunction with *Easy Blues Solos for Guitar*, provides the most comprehensive blues method for the beginning guitarist. Additionally, both of these books provide a preparatory for the *Easy Blues Songbook* which puts together all of the tools necessary for the guitarist that is ready to proceed to the next level; that is, forming a band, making a set list, *etc.*

If the blues have found you then the *Easy Blues Method* will help you find your voice to truly express yourself.

Basic Tablature and Standard Notation

The music in this book has been written in both guitar *tablature* and standard notation. The tablature system has had a long history dating back to the lute music of the Renaissance. Today's TAB system uses six horizontal lines; each line represents a string of the guitar, with string 1 being the highest and string 6 the lowest. The numbers that appear on our TAB staff indicate the fret position, while a zero indicates that the string should be played open.

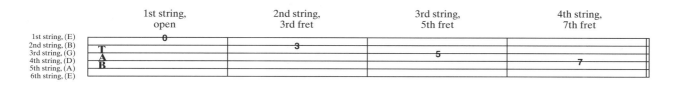

Tablature will only give you the pitch—you have to look at the standard notation to determine the duration of each note. Refer to the chart below for a breakdown of note values.

Chord and Scale Frames

The frames used to illustrate chords and scales are fairly easy to read. The frame depicts a portion of the guitar's fretboard. The vertical lines represent the strings of the guitar with the thickest string to the left and the thinnest to the right. The horizontal lines represent the frets. The nut of the guitar is represented by the bold horizontal line at the top of the diagram. If the top line is not bold then the frame represents a section of the middle of the fretboard with the exact location indicated by the fret number to the right of the frame. The dots that appear in the frames illustrate where you should place your fingers. An **X** above the top line indicates that that string should be muted or not played while an **O** above the top line indicates that that string should be played open.

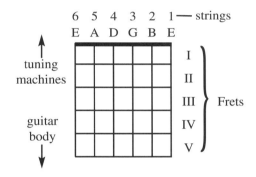

How to Use This Book

The purpose of this book/CD method is to teach you about basic blues rhythm guitar playing. All of the examples are played with a backing band and there is a practice track for you to play along. The practice track has a rhythm guitar, bass guitar, and drums. These tracks provide you with the opportunity to practice in a "live" atmosphere.

Q: How do you learn how to play with a band without playing with a band?
A: By practicing with a band. Even the beginner examples are recorded with a band so you'll be learning how to play in a live situation right from the start.

Listen to the CD and follow along with your book. You can then practice with the example as it's playing or practice with the backup track provided at the end of each section. Each example has a count off so that you'll know when to start playing. Set the backup track to repeat and play as long as you like. Either way you'll be learning as you play and playing as you learn.

The techniques outlined in this book are the basics of blues rhythm vocabulary. The ideas progress gradually. As you learn a new riff you're reinforcing ideas that you had previously learned.

I devised this method when I was first learning how to play. The first thing that I did was to play a rhythm guitar part with a metronome and then record that to a cassette deck. Needless to say, the backup tracks sounded rather boring. Later on I graduated to a four-track recorder and a drum machine. Finally, I had developed the technique and confidence to play with other musicians and attend open blues jams.

The following section, "Crash Course on Music Theory," takes you through all of the musical jargon necessary to fully understand the topics covered in this book and to communicate with other musicians. Those of you who are familiar with these concepts may wish to briefly scan the section while others new to music should study the section thoroughly.

Most of the examples are in the key of A. A was chosen for three reasons: the open strings, it is a popular blues key, and it falls comfortably in the middle of the neck. However, in order to fully understand the concepts presented in this book and develop good technique, it is strongly suggested that practice these techniques in all twelve keys.

Crash Course on Music Theory

Some of you may be new to music, so before going any further let's discuss some basics. Music is a language and the better you understand the fundamental concepts of the language, the better you can communicate.

First, let's look at the musical alphabet. The staff below illustrates the notes available on the guitar.

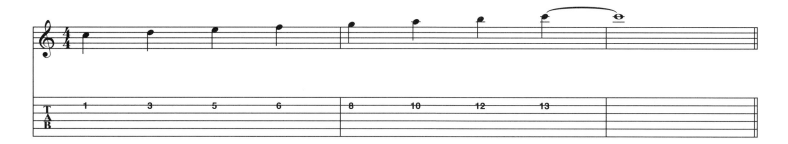

Notice that the letters that make up the note names repeat after every seven notes. The lowest note is an E which moves up to F and then up to G. At this point we go up again to the next note, which is A and the notes that ascend from this point on go up alphabetically from A to G. This cycle repeats itself until we run out of notes on the guitar.

Scales

The notes move up in a series of steps to form a *scale*. A *whole step* is the distance between two notes that are two frets apart, and a *half step* is the distance between any two adjacent notes. Take a look at the following example and notice that as the notes on the musical staff go up, so do the numbers on the tablature staff.

By changing the combination of whole steps and half steps we can change the scale type. We'll use the C major scale as our reference point. The chart below illustrates the scale with whole numbers and Roman numerals.

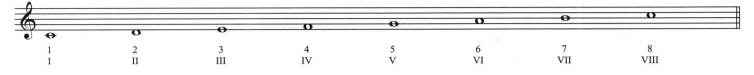

| 1 | 2 | 3 | 4 | 5 | 6 | 7 | 8 |
| I | II | III | IV | V | VI | VII | VIII |

The regular whole numbers refer to the *scale degrees*, or the notes themselves; for example, in the key of C major, scale degree 2 refers to the D note, scale degree 5 refers to the G note, scale degree seven refers to the B note, *etc.* The distance between two notes, or one scale degree to another, is called an *interval*. The Roman numerals refer to chords.

Chords

A *chord* is made up of two or more notes played simultaneously. For example, a *C major triad* is made up of three notes; those three notes are scale degrees 1, 3, and 5—or notes C, E, and G.

Arpeggios

An *arpeggio* is simply a chord that has been broken into single notes.

Power Chords and Diads

Power chords and *diads* are two-note chords used in blues and rock. The ones that we'll be dealing with are fifth, sixth, and seventh chords. For instance, a C5 diad is made up of scale degrees 1 and 5 (or notes C and G). A C6 diad is made up of scale degrees 1 and 6 (or notes C and A). A C7 diad is made up of scale degrees 1 and ♭7 (or notes C and B♭). These chord types are important for playing shuffle rhythms.

Progressions

A *progression* is a chord sequence or pattern. Just like two or more notes make up a chord, two or more chords make up a progression. In blues music a progression is commonly made up of chords I, IV, and V. In the key of C these chords would be C, F, and G. In this book most of the examples are in the key of A. The I, IV, and V chords in the key of A are A, D, and E.

Chord Charts and Leadsheets

Take a look at the diagram below.

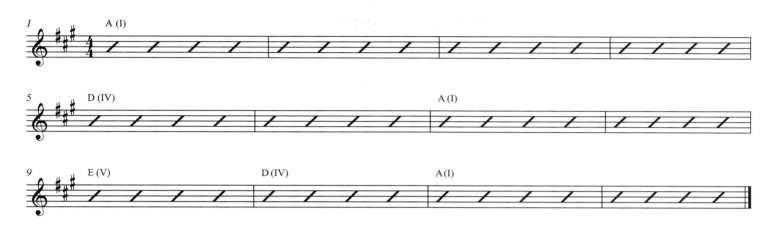

This is called a *chord chart*. It is very important to learn how to read these charts as they can guide you rather painlessly through an entire tune. Although this is just a basic twelve-bar blues progression, the chart helps you visualize what you should be playing.

The following chart contains some more complex notation but don't let that intimidate you.

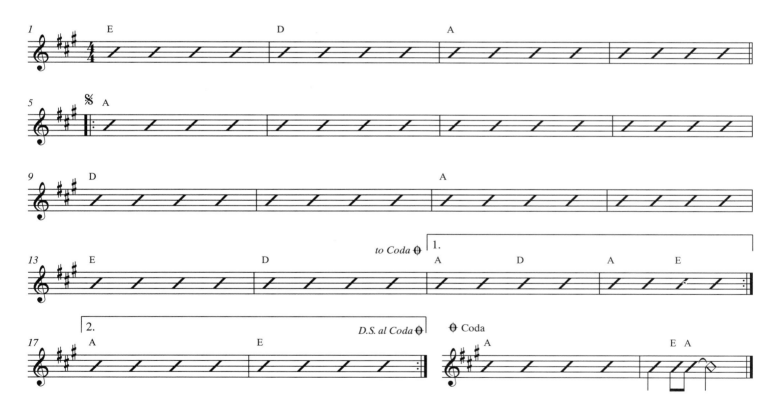

Now, let's go through the chart one step at a time:

- The *intro* consists of the first four *measures* or *bars*.
- The repeat sign (‖:) tells us that this is the measure that we repeat from when we reach this other repeat sign (:‖).
- Notice the twelve measures between repeat signs. This section is called the *verse* or *chorus*. In blues, these terms are interchangeable.
- The rhythm slashes that appear in each measure indicate that a rhythm pattern is being played but does not indicate a specific rhythm.
- The *first* and *second endings* indicate which ending to take depending on how many times you've played the section.
- The last two bars in a twelve-bar blues verse are often referred to as the turnaround. The *turnaround* is a descending (or ascending) pattern played at the end of a blues verse that brings you back to the top.
- The *segno* is the symbol (𝄋). *D.S. al Coda⊕ (Dal Segno al Coda)* indicates that you go back to the 𝄋, replay the section and then to the Coda (⊕).
- This symbol (‖) indicates the end of the tune.

A *leadsheet* is basically the same as a chord chart except that it includes the melody and the lyrics of the tune.

Before we begin playing, please refer to the "Tuning Track" on the CD and tune up. You may use an electronic tuner as all of the examples have been tuned to A=440.

Let's learn how to play the blues. . .

(3) Part I: Basic Rhythms and Rests

Read the "Basic Tablature and Standard Notation" section to familiarize yourself with note values.

Each example is nine measures in length. You'll notice that there is a count off at the beginning letting you know that we're about to start playing. You should keep counting to yourself as you play these exercises.

Learning how to play and count at the same time is very important. You may want to practice clapping the rhythms while you count out loud before you play the exercise. The bold numbers indicate when to play (or clap).

Whole Notes

One whole note equals four beats. Listen to the "count off" and prepare yourself to play on the 1 count and let the note ring for counts 2, 3, and 4. Count to yourself, "**1**, 2, 3, 4, **1**, 2, 3, 4, *etc.*" Notice that the one is emphasized. Play on the bold count.

(4) Example 1

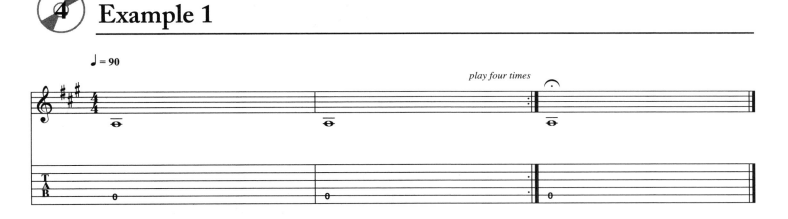

Half Notes

One half note equals two beats. The same basic idea that we just discussed in the previous example still applies. The difference is that you will now be playing on counts 1 and 3. Count to yourself, "**1**, 2, **3**, 4, **1**, 2, **3**, 4, *etc.*"

(5) Example 2

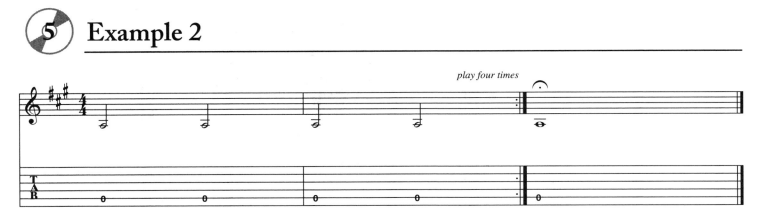

Quarter Notes

One quarter note equals one beat. Here we play on every beat. Count to yourself, "**1, 2, 3, 4, 1, 2, 3, 4,** *etc.*"

6 # Example 3

Eighth Notes

This exercise is very important because all of the patterns in *Part II* are based on this rhythm. In this example there are two notes to every beat (or count). Here we play on and in between the beats. Count to yourself, "**1 &, 2 &, 3 &, 4 &, 1 &, 2 &, 3 &, 4 &,** *etc.*"

7 # Example 4

Whole Notes and Whole Rests

Learning how to play the rests is just as important as learning how to play the notes. Play the note and let it ring for 4 beats then use your fret hand to dampen (or mute) the string by lightly touching it just enough to keep it from ringing. Count to yourself, "**Play, 2, 3, 4, Mute, 2, 3, 4,** *etc.*"

8 # Example 5

Half Notes and Half Rests

Now try playing for 2 beats and muting for 2 beats. Count to yourself, "**Play**, 2, **Mute**, 4, **Play**, 2, **Mute**, 4, *etc.*"

⑨ # Example 6

Quarter Notes and Quarter Rests

Play for 1 beat and mute for 1 beat. Count to yourself, "**Play**, **Mute**, **Play**, **Mute**, **Play**, **Mute**, **Play**, **Mute**, *etc.*"

⑩ # Example 7

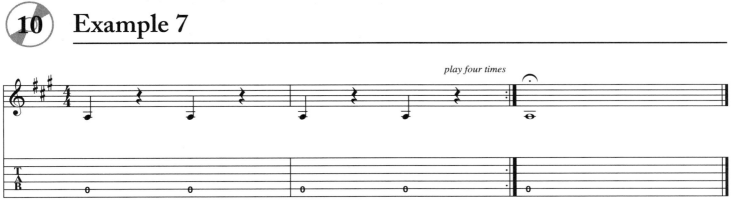

The "Charleston" Rhythm

This exercise is a little tricky as it has a dotted quarter note and eighth note tied to a half note pattern. It sounds more complicated then it actually is, just listen to the CD and I'm sure that you'll get it. Try counting a steady eighth-note pattern to yourself, "**Play** &, 2 **Play**, 3 &, 4 &, **Play** &, 2 **Play**, 3 &, 4 &, *etc.*"

⑪ # Example 8

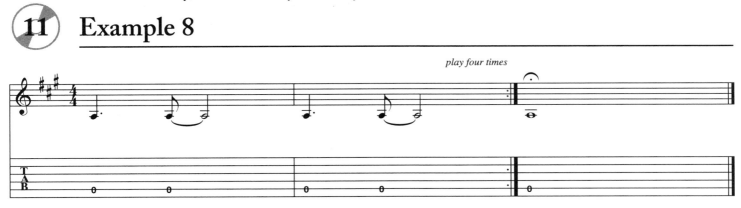

⑫ Practice these exercises steadily until you become comfortable with them. Once you feel that you've gotten used to playing these examples along with the practice track on the CD then you're ready to move along to the next section.

Part II: Open-String Riffs

In this section you'll be playing riffs and boogie patterns based on the eighth-note rhythm exercise from *Part I*. All of the exercises in this section should be played with a swing feel.

What does swing feel mean?
A *swing feel* means that you should play the example with a triplet feel. A *triplet* is when three notes share a beat or count equally. An *eighth-note triplet* is when three eighth notes share a quarter note or one beat. For example, count to yourself, "1 & a, 2 & a, 3 & a, 4 & a, *etc.*" In Example 13 you will see an eighth-note triplet demonstrated on the fourth beat.

So. . . what is swing feel?
Swing feel is when you play two eighth notes instead of three and give the first eighth note the value of the "1 &" count and the second eighth note the value of the "a" count.

You'll notice that the tempo is just a little bit faster (♩ = 100) but the same principles still apply. All of the exercises are in the key of A; that is, they're played on the fifth or A string.

Let's play some boogie patterns. . .

Example 9

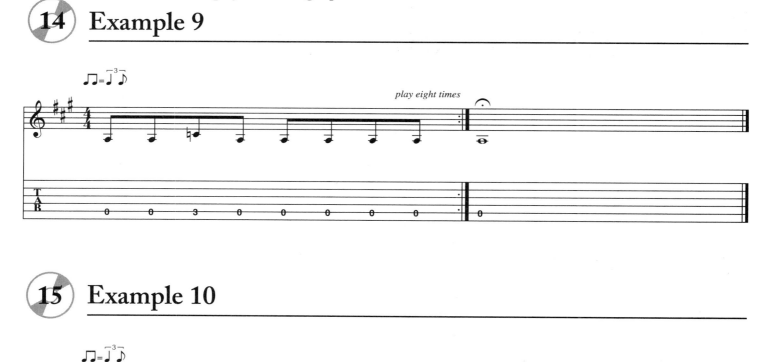

Example 10

16 Example 11

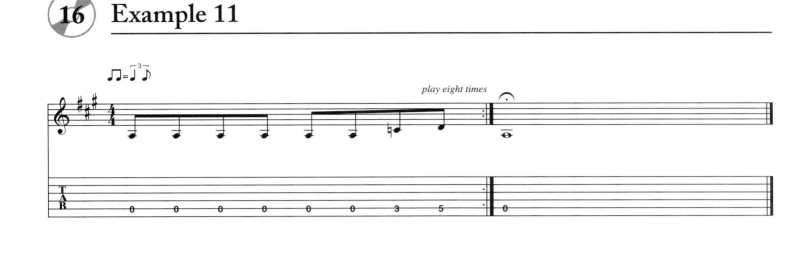

17 Example 12

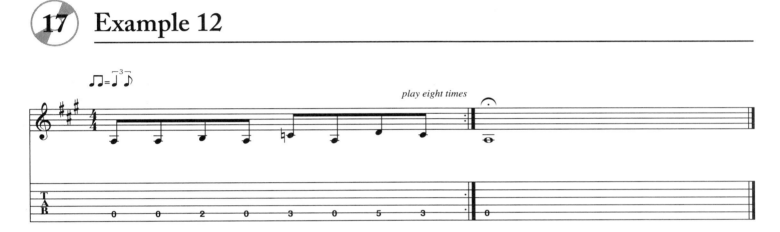

As discussed earlier Example 13 contains an eighth-note triplet, but what I didn't tell you is that it is played as a hammeron. A *hammeron* is when you play the first note by striking the string with your pick and then pressing deliberately with the other finger(s) of the fret hand to produce the sound. Notice the slur marking over the eighth-note triplet. This indicates a hammeron. Listen to the track on the CD and notice how smooth the eighth-note triplet sounds.

18 Example 13

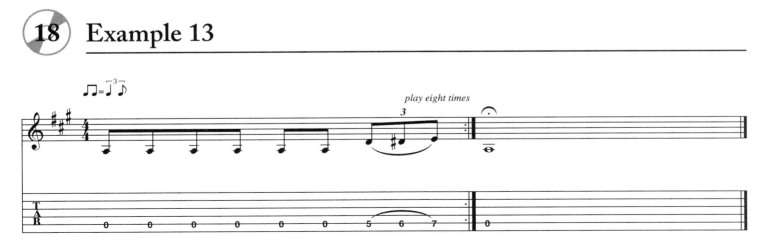

18

 Example 14

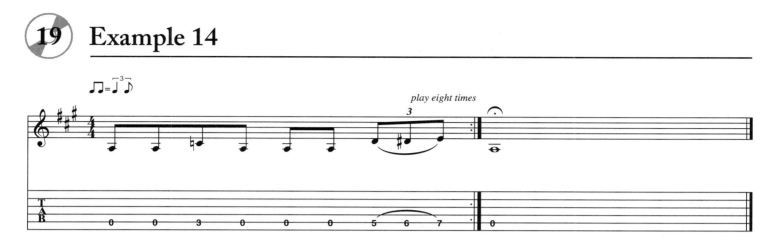

 Example 15

21 **Example 16**

The following exercise includes tied eighth notes. Notice that by using this technique we add a new dimension to the previous examples. Be careful to keep the rhythm steady as you play the tied eighth notes.

22 Example 17

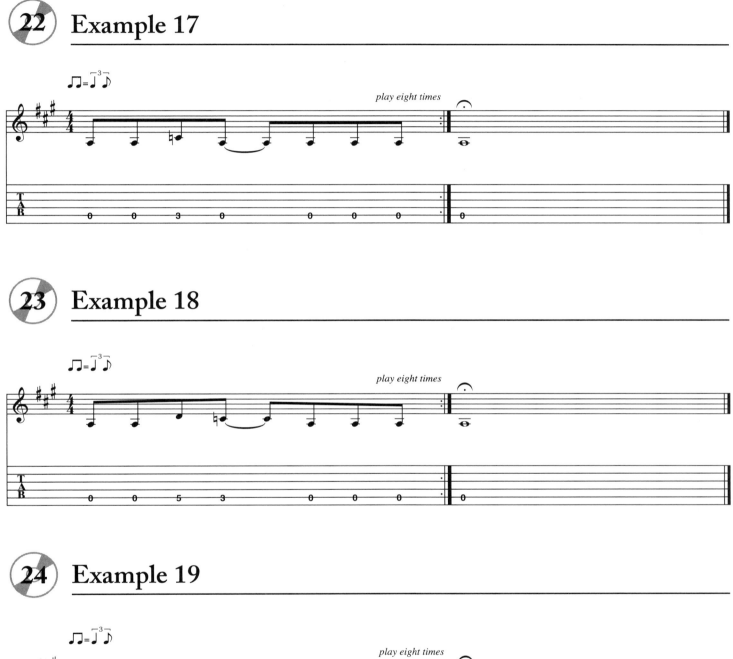

23 Example 18

24 Example 19

This is where the real fun begins: tied eighth notes and an eighth-note triplet.

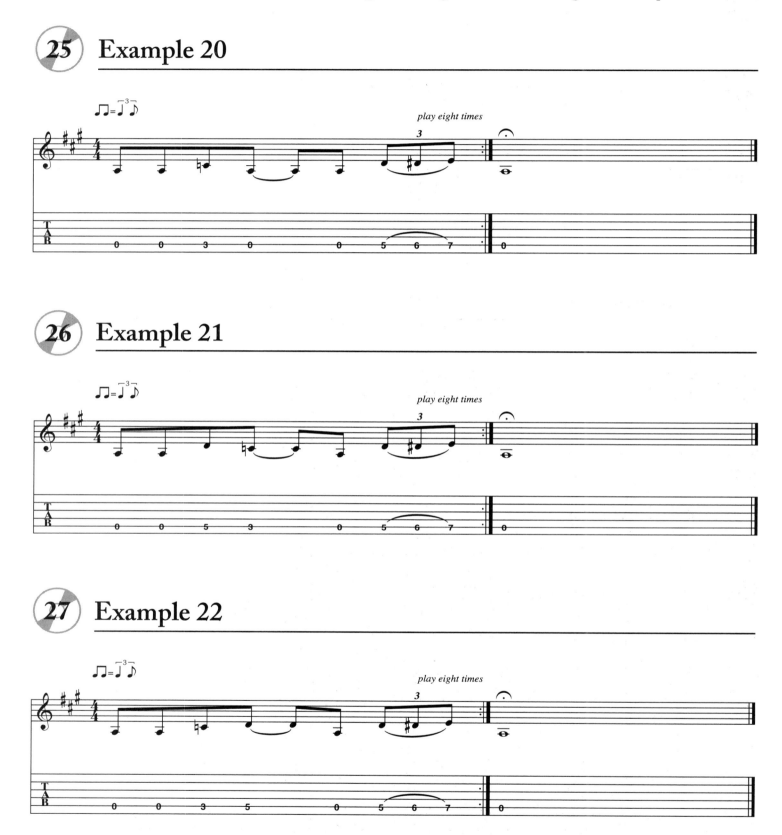

The last example in this section is a popular boogie pattern that also serves as a four-finger exercise. It's best to play this exercise using alternate picking. *Alternate picking* is playing the notes by switching between downstrokes and upstrokes. Since each note is played twice simply play the note first with a downstroke and then with an upstroke.

28 # Example 23

The following examples are played on the fourth or D string. These exercises are the same as the previous ones in this section which is why they are not demonstrated on the CD. They have been included for your reference. Same principles as before apply.

Example 24

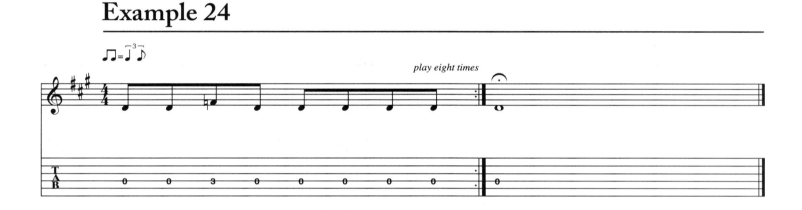

Example 25

Example 26

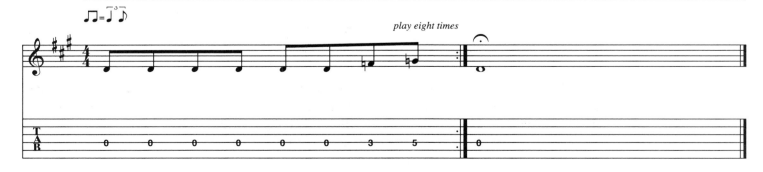

Example 27

Example 28

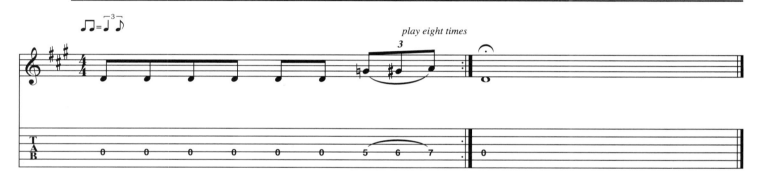

Example 29

Example 30

Example 31

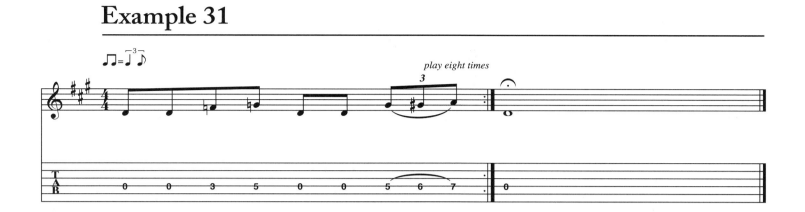

Example 32

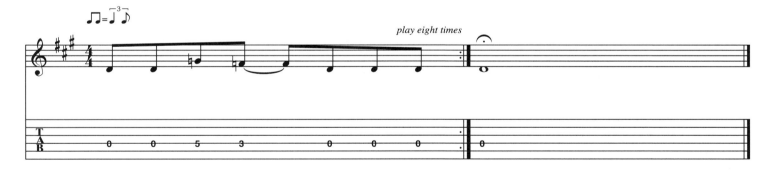

Example 33

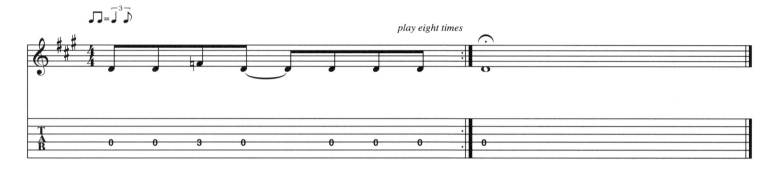

Example 34

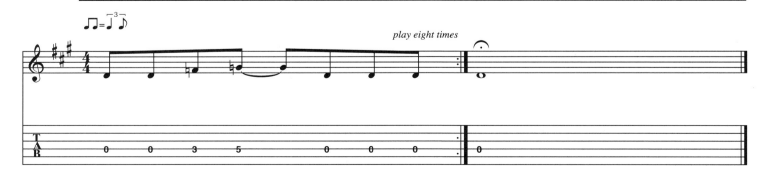

Example 35

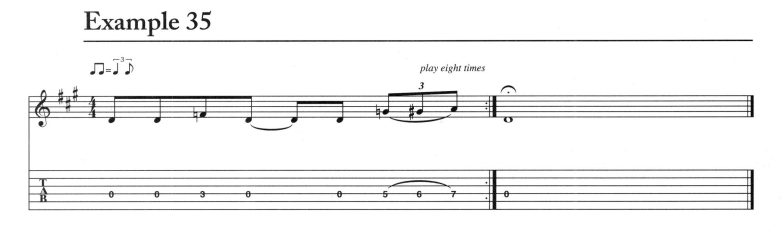

Example 36

Example 37

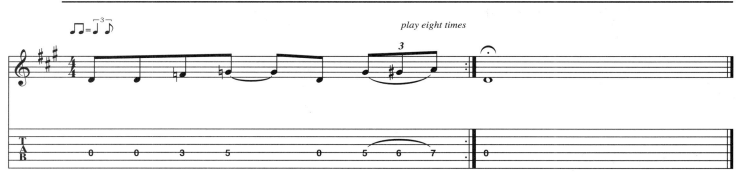

Example 38

Example 39

Example 40

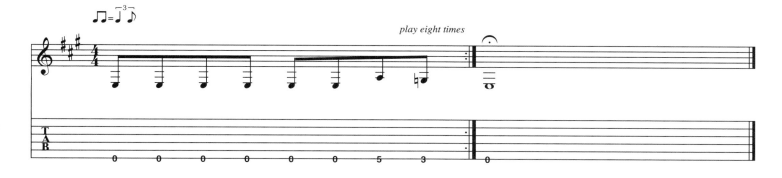

Example 41

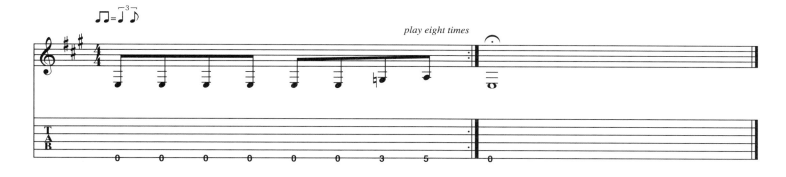

Example 42

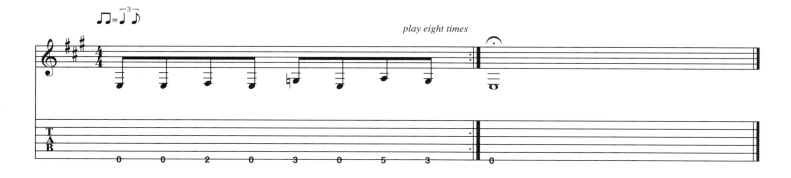

Example 43

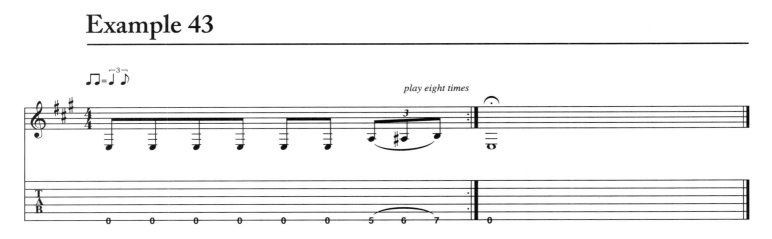

Example 44

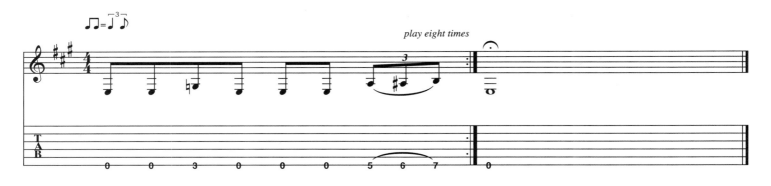

Example 45

Example 46

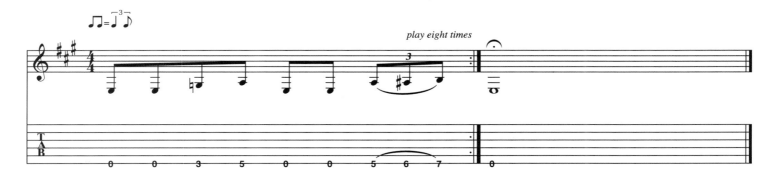

Example 47

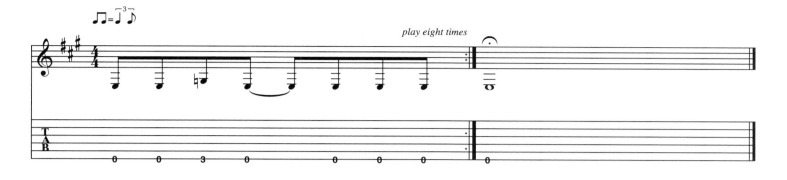

Example 48

Example 49

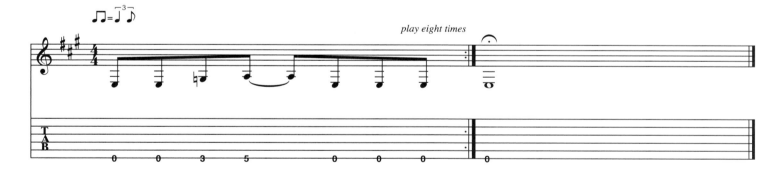

Example 50

Example 51

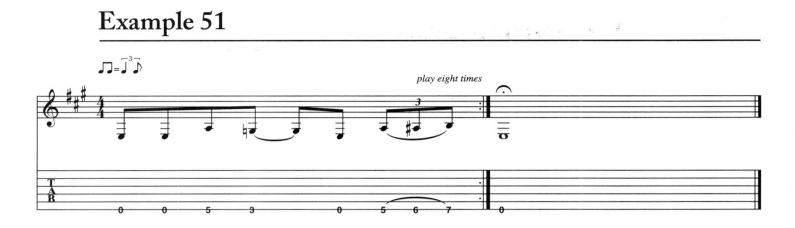

Example 52

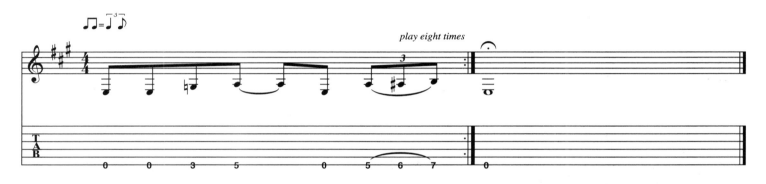

Example 53

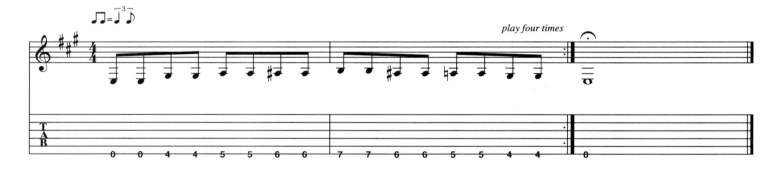

Part III: Turnarounds and Endings

Turnarounds occur at the end of a section (usually the last two measures) and bring you into the next section. As its name implies, a turnaround riff adds motion and turns around or leads into the next verse, chorus, or bridge.

Endings are self-explanatory and indicate the completion of a song.

In this section both turnarounds and endings are demonstrated in the same example. The first two measures are the turnaround and the third or last measure is the ending.

The following exercises show you five different ways of playing turnarounds and endings for the same song. Notice that the bass doubles the guitar during the turnaround and ending.

Example 54

Example 55

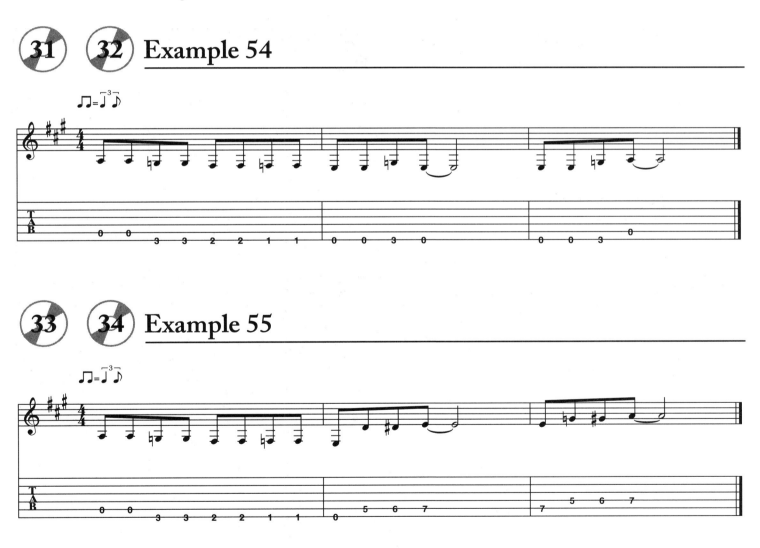

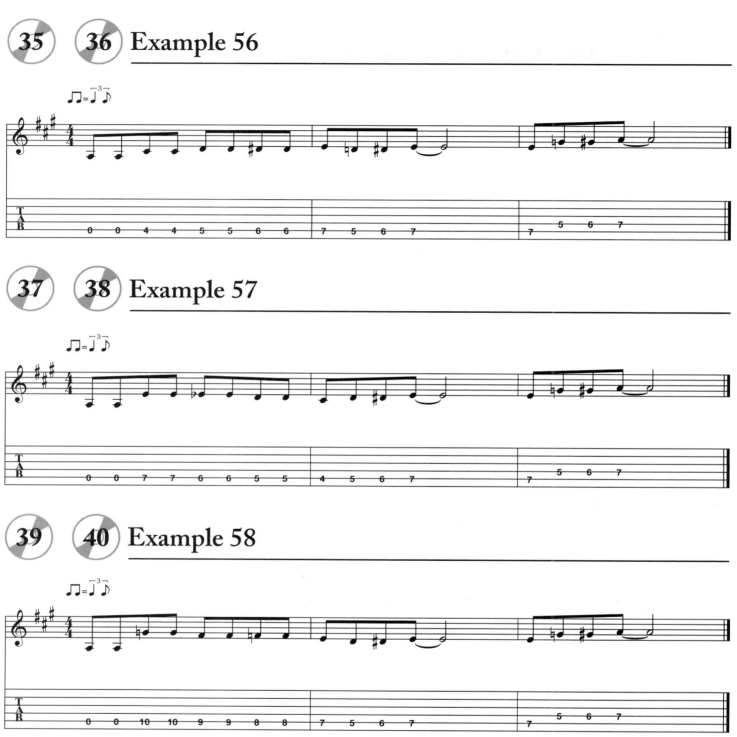

You can also substitute the last measure with the second measure for a more abrupt ending. These combination turnaround/ending riffs are usually discussed beforehand; however, more advanced players can "improvise" these ending riffs with subtle eye contact or, if possible, hand gestures.

Once you memorize these riffs you can recall them in a live band situation with confidence.

(41) Part IV: Two-Note Chord Patterns

Now that we have some open-string riffs under our belt, it's time to move into the wonderful world of chord playing. A *chord* is simply two or more notes played simultaneously. In this section we'll demonstrate some two-note chord patterns and riffs. There are ten examples in total and the following are demonstrated with a swing feel

(42) Example 59

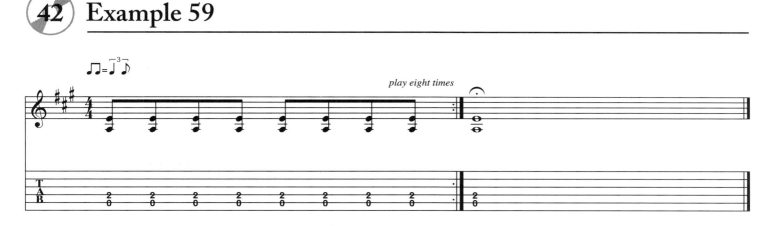

This next example was made popular by Chuck Berry and is sometimes referred to as "chuckin'."

(43) Example 60

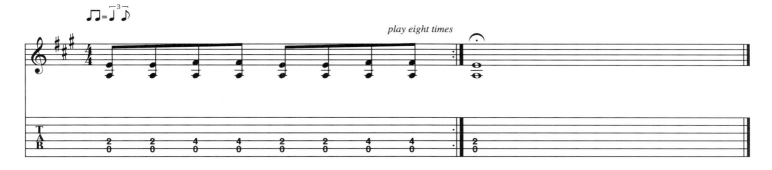

Here we see a variation on the "chuckin'" example by walking up and back from the next note.

(44) Example 61

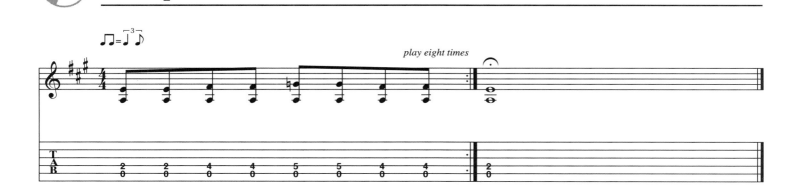

The following two examples are variations of the previous two. Here we revisit the eighth-note triplet on the fourth beat. Notice the hammeron between the first two notes of the triplet.

45 Example 62

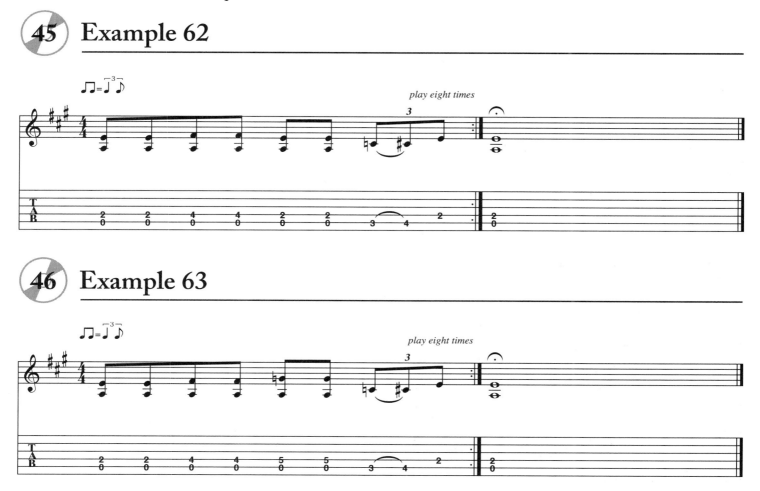

Now, notice the difference with the eighth-note triplet on beat four. To play this example you need to catch the top two strings with an upstroke as you prepare to play the first note of the next measure. Don't worry too much about playing exactly the top two notes. These exercises are more of a feel thing. Notice how the scratch bounces you into the next measure.

47 Example 64

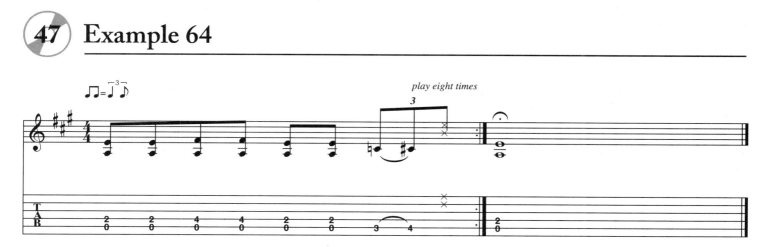

48 **Example 65**

Remember the tied eighth note and eighth-note triplet examples in *Part II*. It's even more fun with chords.

49 **Example 66**

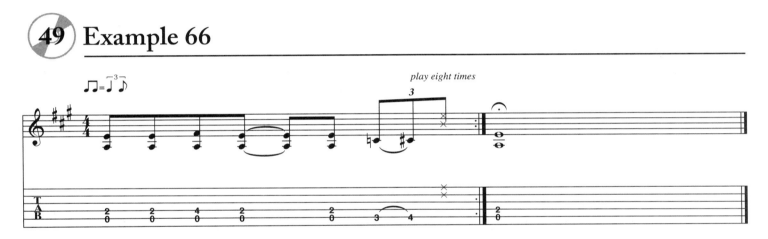

Notice the slight bend on the fifth string/third fret C natural note. The slight bend gives it a little extra bluesy feel.

50 **Example 67**

The following example is also known as a "Texas Boogie." Playing the chords on the off-beats gives this example an immediately recognizable rhythmic drive. This groove is a lot of fun to play but take your time with it because it's really easy to rush those offbeat hits. If you have a hard time with the last two chords in the exercise then try playing just the notes on the fifth string until you get the hang of it.

(51) Example 68

Below you'll find the previous examples written for the D chord. As before these examples are not demonstrated on the CD.

Example 69

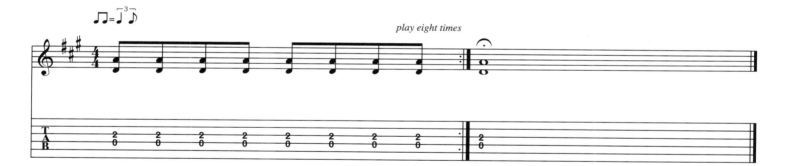

Example 70

Example 71

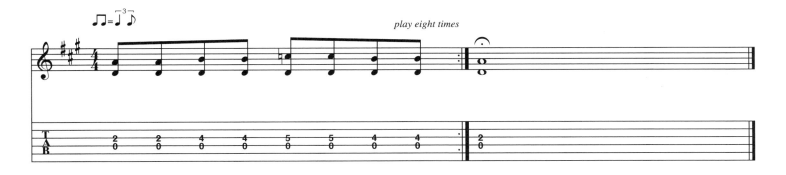

Example 72

Example 73

Example 74

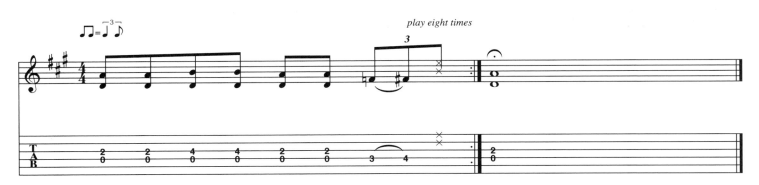

Example 75

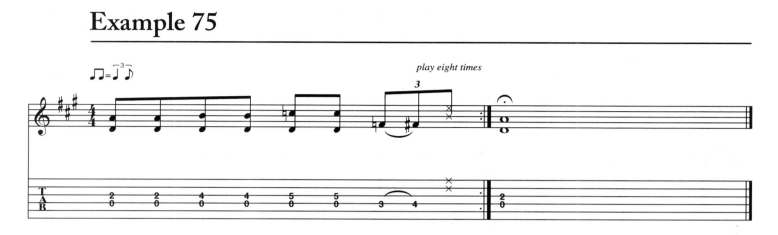

Example 76

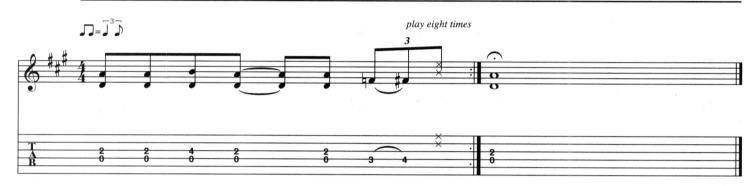

Example 77

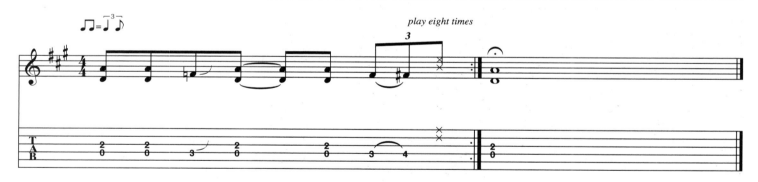

Example 78

. . . And written for the E chord. As before these examples are not demonstrated on the CD.

Example 79

Example 80

Example 81

Example 82

Example 83

Example 84

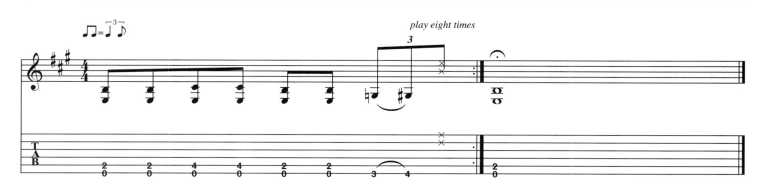

Example 85

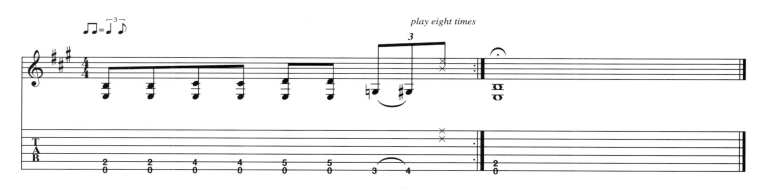

Example 86

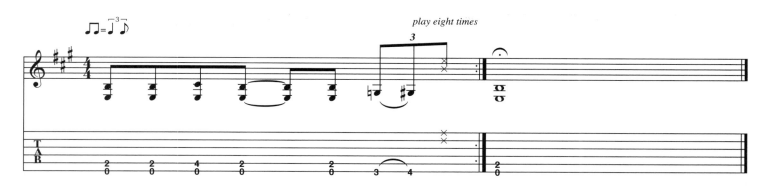

Example 87

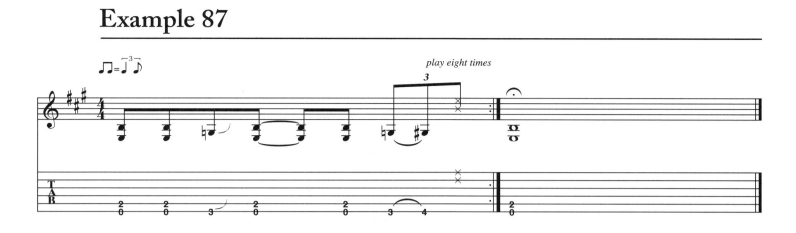

Example 88

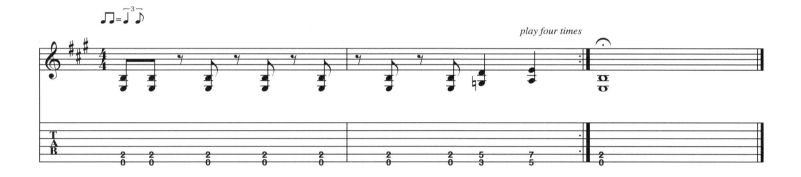

The following exercises are the same as the previous examples in this section except that they are played with a rock or straight-eighth feel. *Rock* or *straight-eighth feel* simply means that the eighth notes are played evenly. Notice the different ending.

Also take note that these examples are to be played with a palm mute. A *palm mute* is a technique in which you rest the palm of your picking hand on the low strings near the bridge of the guitar. This gives the chords a thick and chunky sound. Check it out!

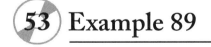

Example 89

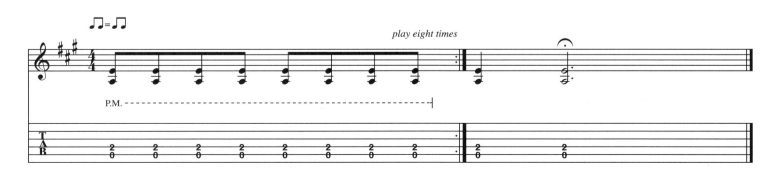

54 Example 90

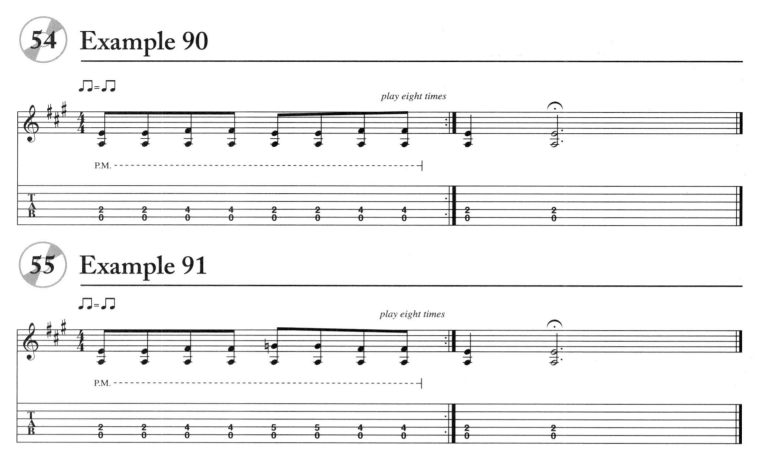

55 Example 91

The eighth-note triplet on the fourth beat has now been replaced by two sixteenths and an eighth. A sixteenth note is half of an eighth note. Try counting sixteenth notes like this, "1 e & a, 2 e & a, 3 e & a, 4 e & a, *etc.*" Now try counting this example, "1 &, 2 &, 3 &, 4 e & a, *etc.*"

56 Example 92

57 Example 93

58 Example 94

59 Example 95

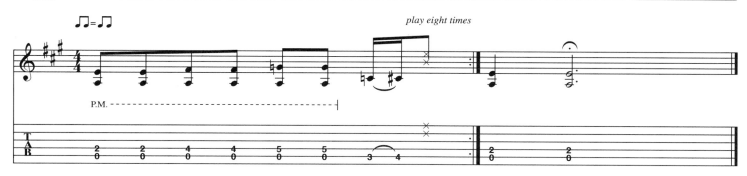

60 Example 96

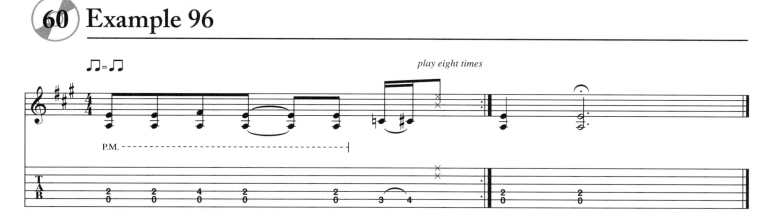

61 Example 97

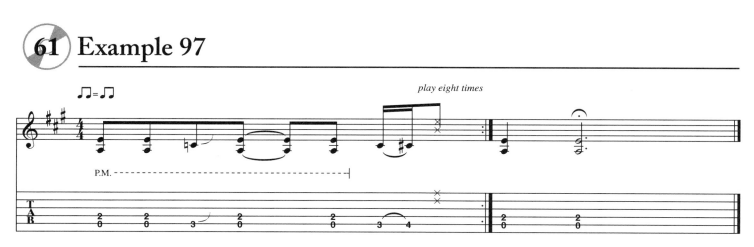

The "Texas Boogie" exercise works nicely with a rock feel. . .

62 Example 98

D chord examples with a rock feel. (Not on CD)

Example 99

Example 100

Example 101

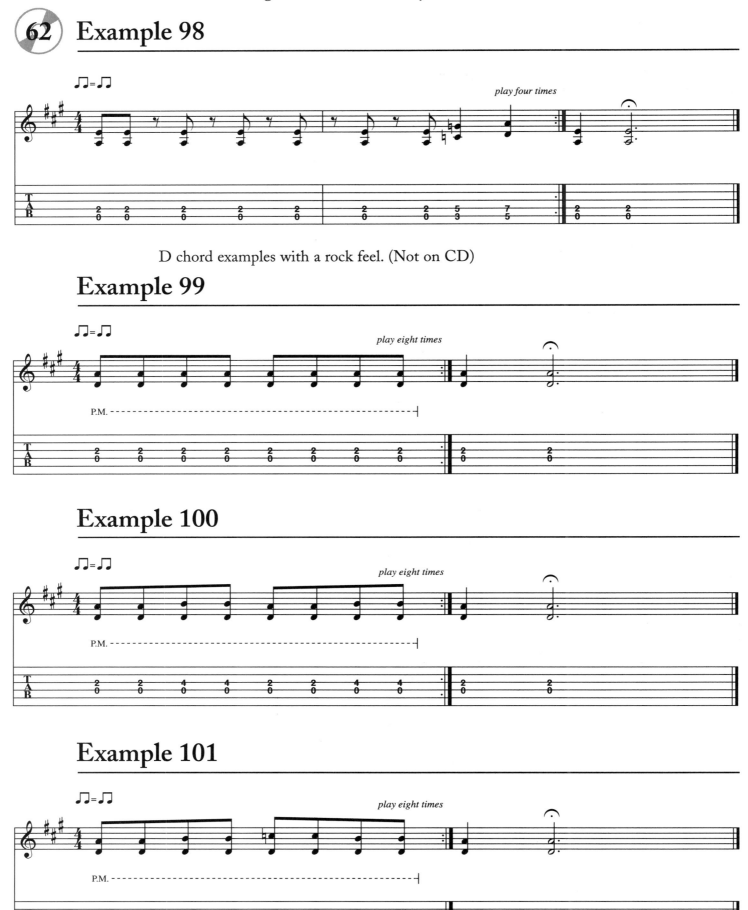

Example 102

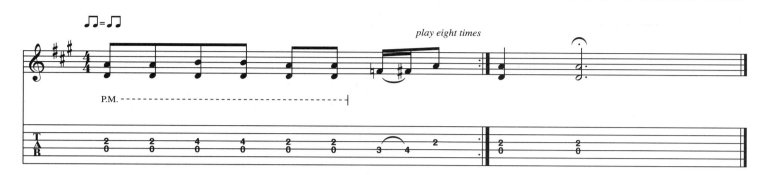

Example 103

Example 104

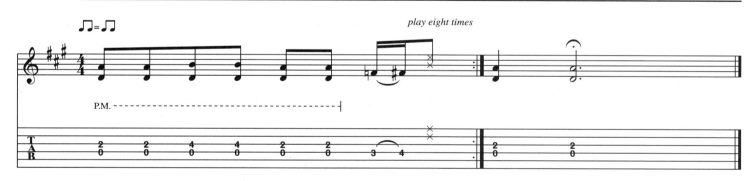

Example 105

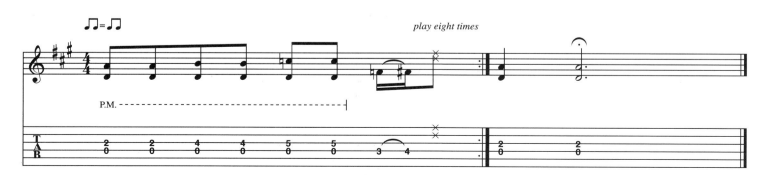

44

Example 106

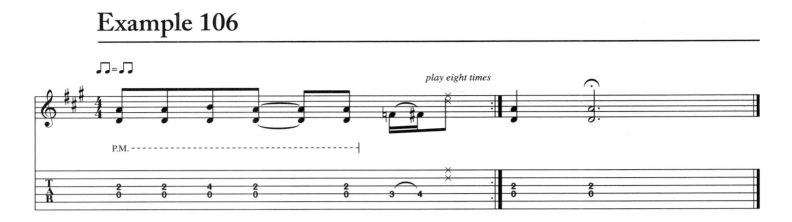

Example 107

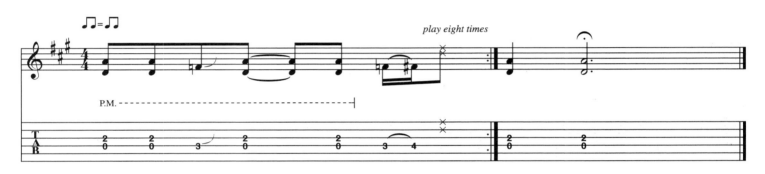

Example 108

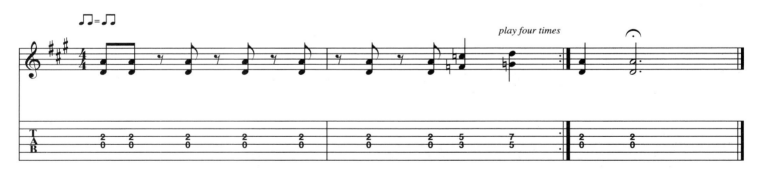

E chord examples with a rock feel. (Not on CD)

Example 109

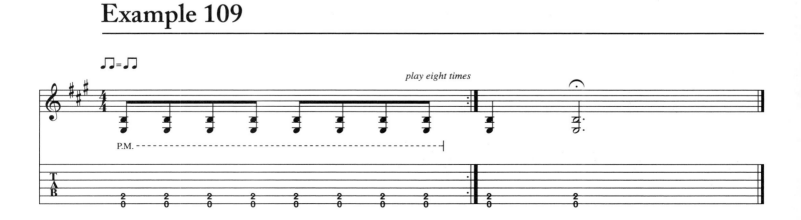

Example 110

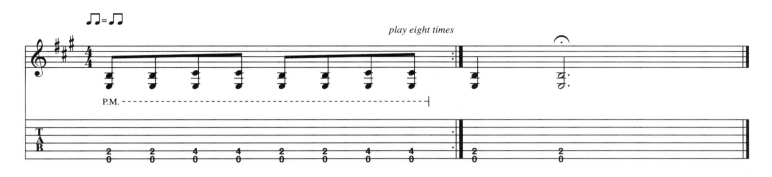

Example 111

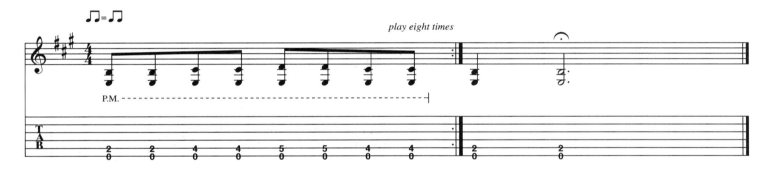

Example 112

Example 113

Example 114

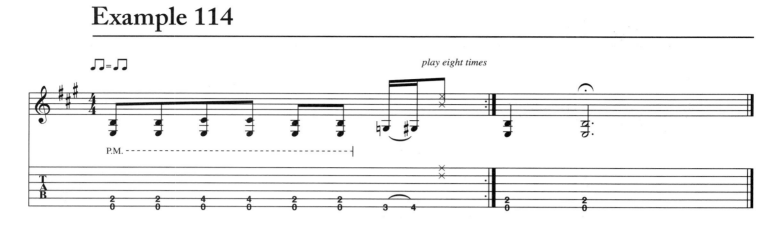

Example 115

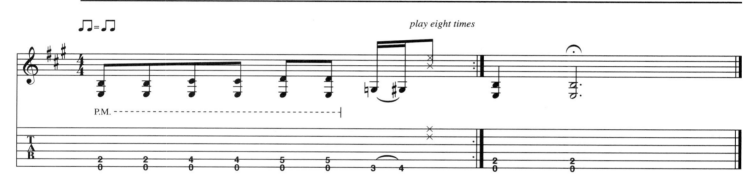

Example 116

Example 117

Example 118

Part V: Putting It All Together

Let's take a look at what we've learned so far:
- Rhythms and Rests
- Open-String Boogie Riffs
- Turnarounds and Endings
- Two-Note Chord Patterns

In this section we're going to put it all together and start playing songs. We'll begin by reviewing the open-string boogie patterns that we discussed in *Part II*. Next, we'll practice moving them from one string to another or, more correctly, from one chord to the next.

Once you're comfortable moving these patterns from one string to another then you're ready to start playing the following examples.

There is also a new technique that we're going to introduce. Take a look at measure 4 and notice that the boogie pattern is different in this measure. Once again you'll be using alternate picking to "walk up" from the A (I chord) to the D (IV chord). This riff is called a *walkup*.

Let's take a look at the 12-bar blues pattern of the following songs:
- We have a count off and a drum fill for the Intro.
- The verse is 12 bars (or measures) that break down as follows four bars of A (remember that the walkup in bar 4 is part of the A chord), two bars of D, followed by 2 bars of A. The last four bars get a little tricky: one bar of E, one bar of D, one bar of A, and one bar of E.

More simply;

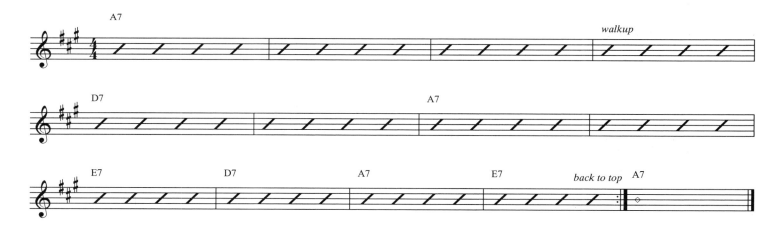

- Notice the drum fill during the E chord in measure 12. This brings us into the next section or 12-bar verse.
- And finally, another drum fill over the E chord in measure 24 indicating the end of the song.

The tempo is also a little bit faster (♩ = 110) making these song examples more challenging, interesting, and fun. Try to be aware of what's ahead so that you can make each transition smoothly and easily. Be careful not to rush. Remember, this is what we've been working towards.

Now, enjoy!

65 Example 119

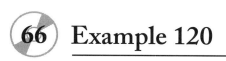

Example 120

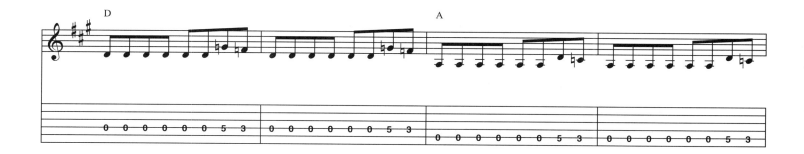

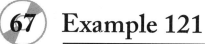

Example 121

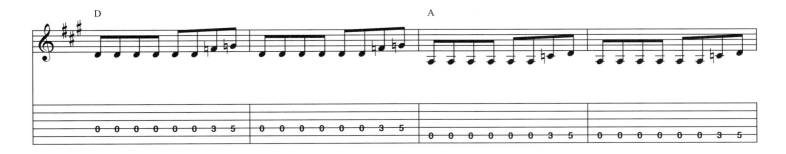

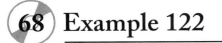

68 # Example 122

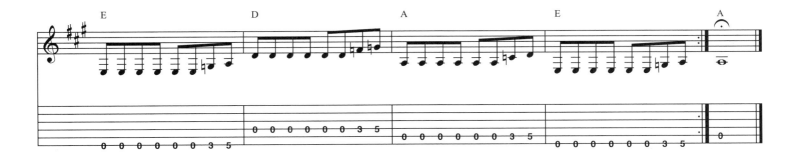

69 Example 123

70 Example 124

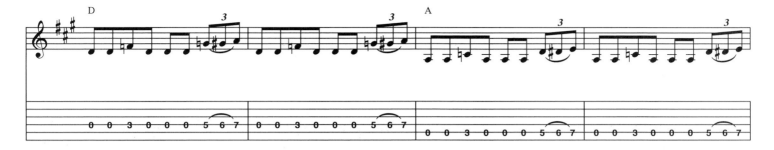

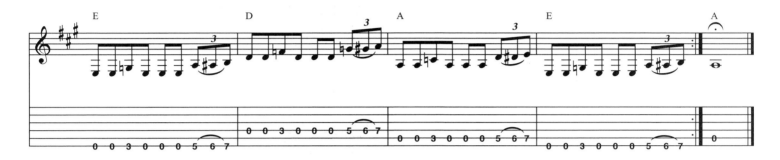

71 Example 125

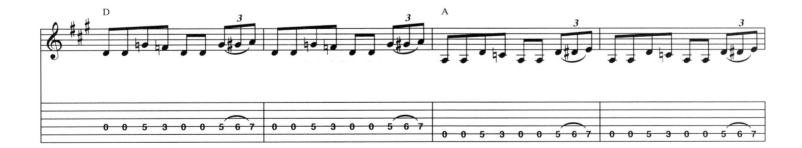

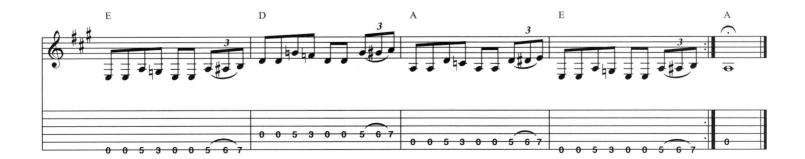

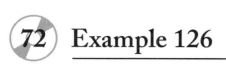

Example 126

Example 127

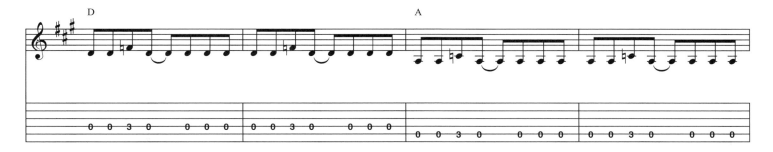

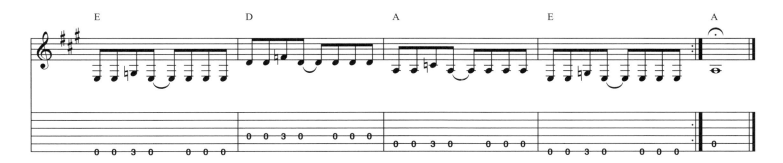

74 Example 128

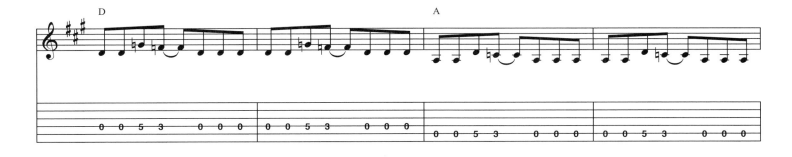

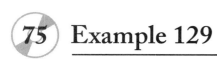 **Example 129**

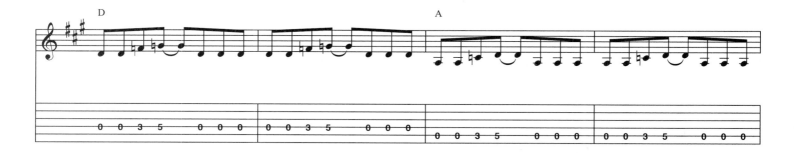

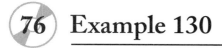 **Example 130**

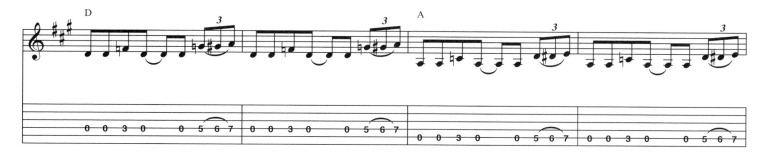

77 Example 131

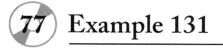

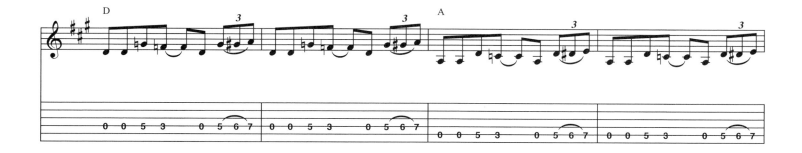

Example 132

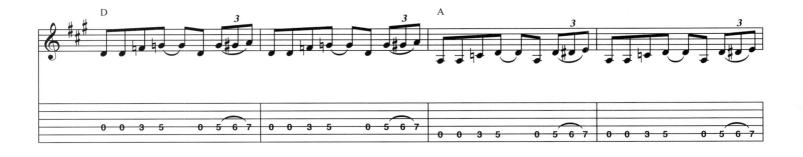

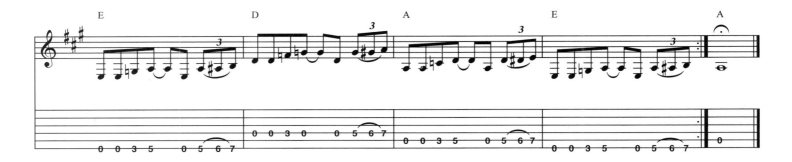

The next example is a variation of Example 23. It has been modified to fit the 12-bar patterns outlined in this section.

Example 133

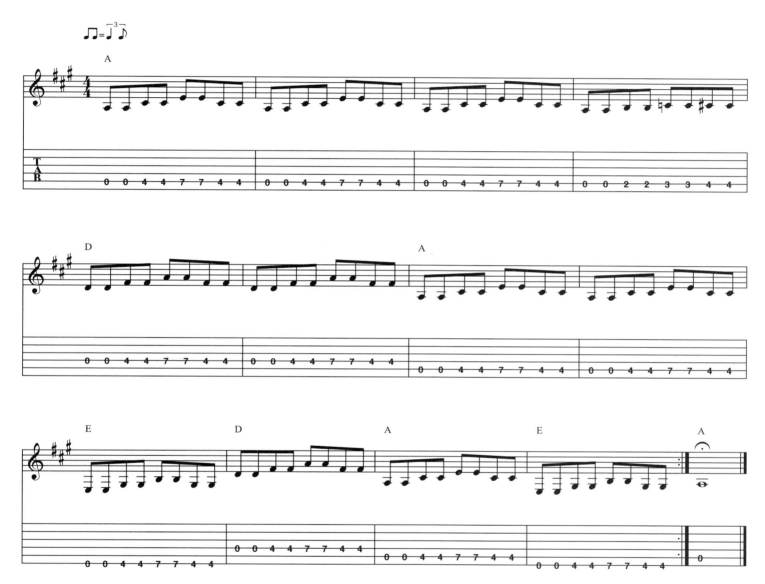

The rhythm guitar in all of the songs is playing Example 60. You can use the backup track to:
- Practice the two-note chord patterns found in Part IV
- Play the examples in this book as written
- Combine different examples
- Or create some of your own

(81) Part VI: Advanced Techniques

You're now ready to play some serious blues rhythm patterns!

Once again the tempo has been raised just a little bit to keep you on your toes. There are six songs in this section and each song has a slightly different feel. Also, please note that each song example has two guitar parts (except for "Swing Blues" which has three guitar parts). The guitars have been arranged so that they complement each other while demonstrating a different technique. Some of these rhythm patterns may be a little awkward at first but with some practice you should have no problem with them.

The beginning of each song is indicated by a count off and a drum fill. Listen to the song track while following along with the music in your book. The guitars are split in the stereo mix making them easily identifiable. Practice along with the song track if you're having difficulty with a particular guitar part. The practice track doesn't include any guitars providing you with your own rhythm section. It is suggested that you use the practice track to play what you've learned or to create your own rhythm parts.

Let's check out the first song. . .

Boogie Blues

This song is played with a swing feel. Guitar 1 is playing a technique known as *sliding sixths*. The interval that separates the two notes that make up this chord is a major sixth. Simply slide into the first two notes on the seventh fret and then slide down two frets to the fifth fret. Try to imitate the horn section of a big band when you use this technique.

Guitar 2 is playing "The Charleston Rhythm" example from *Part I*. Notice the extended chord voicings. (A *voicing* is the arrangement of the notes in a chord.) Blues harmony is based on dominant seven chords. When you "extend" the intervals to those greater than a seventh you get a more complex sound. The 13 and 9 chords give this tune an "uptown" (or more interesting) sound.

82 83 Boogie Blues

Chicago Blues

Play this song with a swing feel. When your playing with other instruments (*i.e.* a piano, horns, or another guitar) it isn't necessary to play big thick chords. Let the music breathe. Guitar 1 is playing a three-note A7 chord with a back-beat groove. *Back beat* refers to beats two and four. This rhythm pattern falls on beats two and four—just listen to the snare drum. Also, the extended harmony of the IV and V chords (D9 and E9) is played on the top three strings. The fifth string is lightly fretted but the chord sound comes from strings one, two, and three.

Guitar 2 demonstrates a chuckin' pattern that you've already played in *Part IV*. The difference being that this guitar part isn't played with open strings. Mastering this rhythm pattern will allow you to play in any key simply by sliding the chord form to any area of the fretboard. You'll also find that you have more control over the chord sound when you're not playing open strings.

Lastly, you can also practice the turnarounds and endings from *Part III* in this song example.

84   85   **Chicago Blues**

Rock Blues

As the title implies, play this song with a rock feel. Guitar 1 plays a big A7 chord with all six strings. The rhythm pattern is a steady eighth-note groove. Strum evenly using alternate picking pressing down with your fret hand on beats one and three. Lighten your fret-hand grip while you're strumming to achieve that scratching sound. This rhythmic pattern adds drive to the song without getting in the other guitar player's way.

Guitar 2 provides a two-note open-string pattern. It's a variation on Example 91. You can also substitute any example from *Part IV* to complement Guitar 1.

86 87 Rock Blues

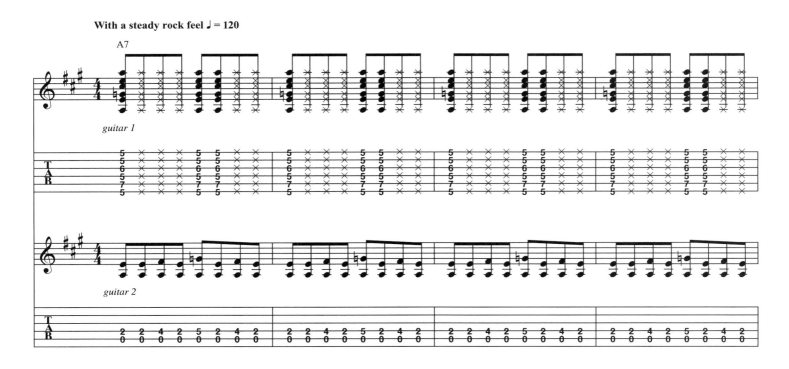

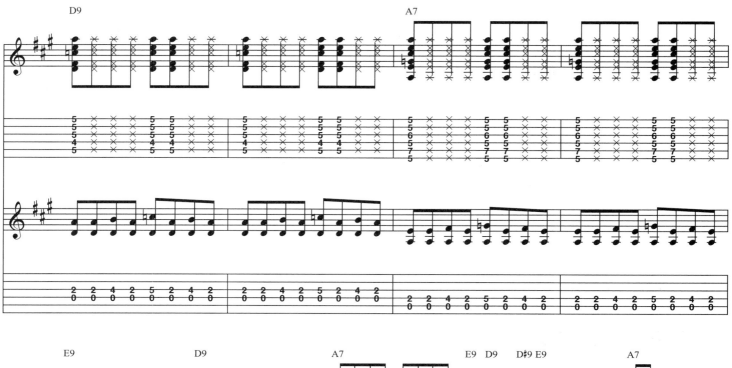
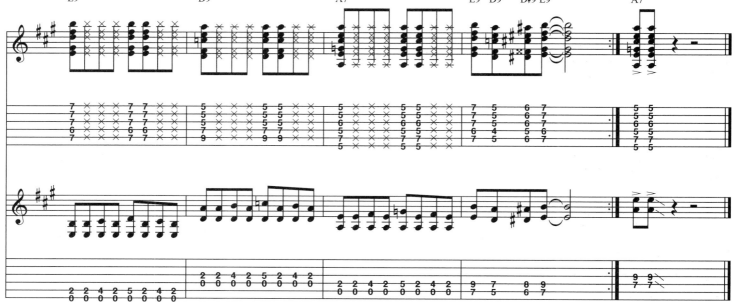

Shuffle Blues

This song has a classic triplet feel. Every blues band has at least one song like this in their set list. Guitar 1 is playing a typical blues riff instead of a chord. The notes, however, outline an A7. Play the notes short or *staccato* with the exception of the triplet on beat four. Notice the hammeron between the first two notes in the triplet.

The three-note chord pattern in Guitar 2 is reminiscent of the sliding sixths that you played in "Boogie Blues." This rhythm pattern also includes a muted scratch that adds drive to the groove. Notice that the walkup (in measure four) can also be executed with chords.

88 89 Shuffle Blues

Moderate shuffle (with a triplet feel) ♩ = 120

Swing Blues

"Swing Blues" is arranged for three guitars and played with a swing feel in the key of B♭. This tune has a very uptown sound. Guitars 1 and 2 demonstrate a *call-and-response* technique. Guitar 1 plays a single-note line that is answered by Guitar 2's two-note chord jabs. Again, think big band: The brass (trumpets and trombones) answering the reeds (saxophones).

Guitars 1 and 2 are anchored by the four-to-the-floor rhythmic pattern played by Guitar 3. *Four-to-the-floor* is a technique made famous by Freddie Green (the guitarist for the Count Basie Orchestra). You simply play the chord using quarter notes and downstrokes. Also, "bounce" your fret hand to play the chords staccato. This technique imitates the sound of a foot thumping on the floor; hence, the name, four-to-the-floor.

Notice that each guitar has room to breathe and all of the instruments are playing off of each other. The music simply sounds like conversation.

The practice track includes Guitar 3. You can practice the call-and-response riffs or create your own riffs.

90 91 Swing Blues

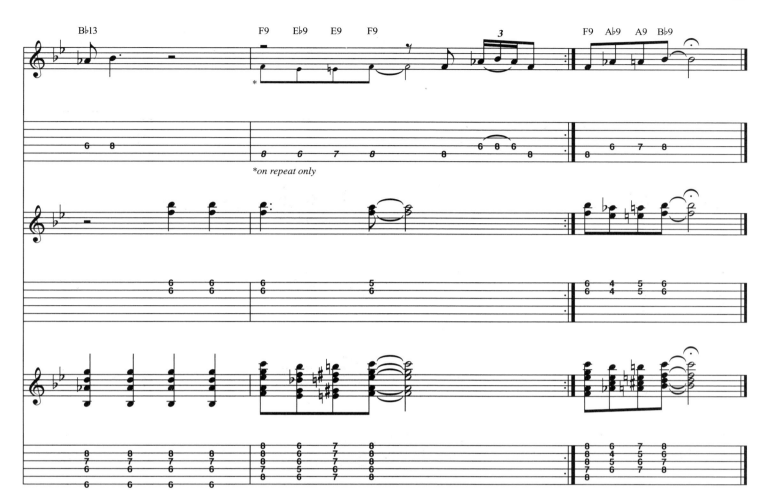

*on repeat only

B.D.'s Blues

I hope you're ready for some fun.

This final tune is a 'tip of the hat' to blues legend Bo Diddley. Guitars 1 and 2 are engaged in a call-and-response riff. Both guitars do come together in measures nine and ten adding a dynamic flavor to the song. The riffs rhythmically imitate each other but the chord shapes are slightly different.

Guitar 1 is played on the top three strings and Guitar 2 is played on the second, third, and fourth strings. This difference in register along with some basic changes in sound give each guitar a recognizably different voice.

This is a very enjoyable groove to play. Don't labor too much over playing the rhythm parts exact—think of it as more of a feel thing.

B.D.'s Blues

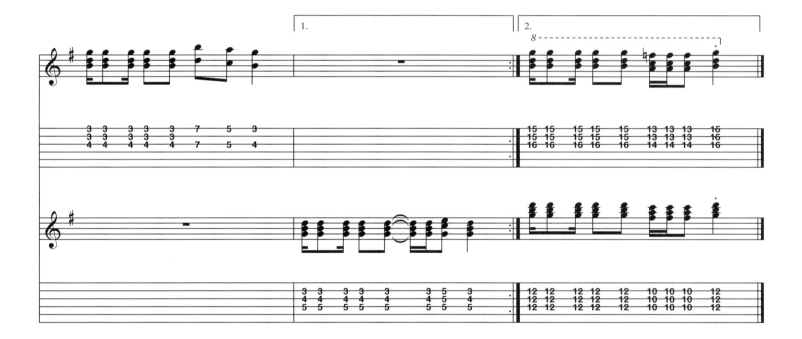

94 In Conclusion

Congratulations! You should now have a solid foundation for blues rhythm guitar playing. At this time you should seek out other players who share the same interest in blues and jam with them, learn from them, and ultimately, become one of them. Find out what blues standards are popular with the local blues players in your area and learn them.

The greatest teachers are the players that you idolize—Stevie Ray Vaughan once said of B.B. King's album *Live at the Regal*, "I go back to that record and it's like a little book. . . there's always something new," and of his record collection, ". . . they're all little books." So take Stevie Ray's advice and listen to as many recordings of your favorite players as possible. Learn the blues straight from the source. Good Luck!

"Everybody's got their own touch. . . nobody has the same touch on guitar."
—Otis Rush

"Listening to the great bluesmen—how they played so well and were so relaxed—really inspired me."
—Stevie Ray Vaughan